Incredibly Insane Sports

RODEO

By Jessica Cohn

Gareth Stevens
Publishing

Please visit our website, www.garethstevens.com. For a free color catalog of all our high-quality books, call toll free 1-800-542-2595 or fax 1-877-542-2596.

Library of Congress Cataloging-in-Publication Data

Cohn, Jessica.

 Rodeo / Jessica Cohn.

     p. cm. — (Incredibly insane sports)

ISBN 978-1-4339-8839-4 (pbk.)

ISBN 978-1-4339-8840-0 (6-pack)

ISBN 978-1-4339-8838-7 (library binding)

1. Rodeos—Juvenile literature. I. Title.

 GV1834.C6 2013

 791.8'4—dc23

                         2012037749

First Edition

Published in 2013 by

Gareth Stevens Publishing

111 East 14th Street, Suite 349

New York, NY 10003

©2013 Gareth Stevens Publishing

Produced by Netscribes Inc.

Art Director Dibakar Acharjee

Editorial Content The Wordbench

Copy Editor Sarah Chassé

Picture Researcher Sandeep Kumar G

Designer Rishi Raj

Illustrators Ashish Tanwar, Indranil Ganguly, Prithwiraj Samat, and Rohit Sharma

Photo credits:

Page no. = #, t = top, a = above, b = below, l = left, r = right, c = center

Front Cover: Shutterstock Images LLC Title Page: Shutterstock Images LLC

Contents Page: Shutterstock Images LLC Inside: Shutterstock Images LLC: 4, 5, 6, 7, 8, 9, 10, 11b, 12t, 12b, 13t, 13cl, 13cr, 14, 15, 16, 17, 18, 19, 20, 21, 22, 23, 24, 25, 26, 27, 28t, 28b, 29, 30, 31, 32, 33, 34, 35, 36, 37, 38, 39, 40, 41, 42, 43.

Printed in the United States of America

CPSIA compliance information: Batch #CW13GS: For further information contact Gareth Stevens, New York, New York at 1-800-542-2595.

Contents

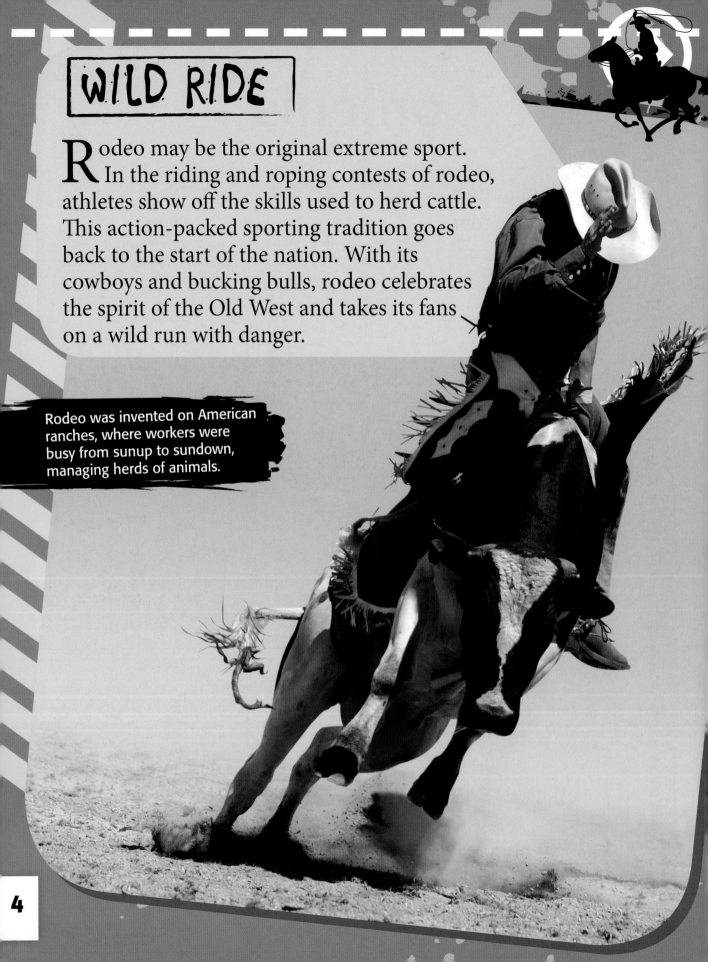

WILD RIDE

Rodeo may be the original extreme sport. In the riding and roping contests of rodeo, athletes show off the skills used to herd cattle. This action-packed sporting tradition goes back to the start of the nation. With its cowboys and bucking bulls, rodeo celebrates the spirit of the Old West and takes its fans on a wild run with danger.

Rodeo was invented on American ranches, where workers were busy from sunup to sundown, managing herds of animals.

Ranching World

American rodeo has caught on in other countries where **livestock** and ranching are important. These rodeo republics include Brazil and Argentina, as well as Australia. In each nation, rodeo has its own style, which comes from the people's traditions. But the basic elements remain the same. The contestants show their skills for riding, for roping animals, and for taking risks.

In calf roping contests, the calf gets a head start, and the contestant tries to rope it.

Steer to Victory

Rodeo is one wild ride after another. In **steer** wrestling, the riders leap from their horses and grab a steer by the head. This is also called bulldogging. The contestants must try to stop the animal, with their own strength, in just a few seconds.

Team roping is a two-person skill. The person who is the header ropes the steer's head. The heeler ropes the animal's legs. In tie-down roping, a rider ropes a running calf and then jumps from his or her horse to tie the calf's legs together with a second rope.

Team roping is also called heading and heeling.

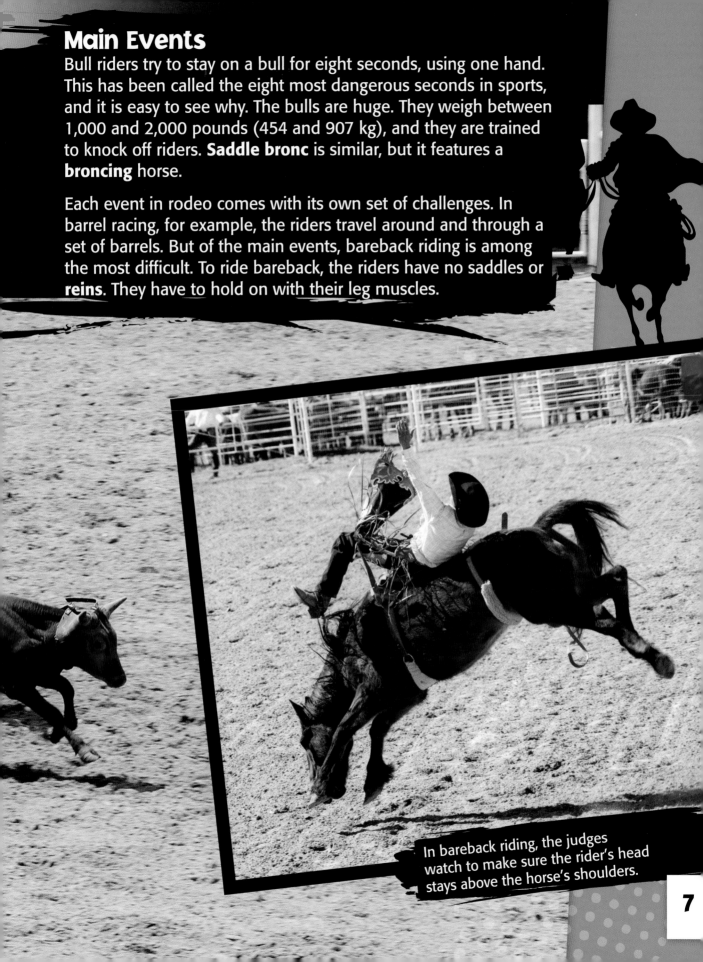

Main Events

Bull riders try to stay on a bull for eight seconds, using one hand. This has been called the eight most dangerous seconds in sports, and it is easy to see why. The bulls are huge. They weigh between 1,000 and 2,000 pounds (454 and 907 kg), and they are trained to knock off riders. **Saddle bronc** is similar, but it features a **broncing** horse.

Each event in rodeo comes with its own set of challenges. In barrel racing, for example, the riders travel around and through a set of barrels. But of the main events, bareback riding is among the most difficult. To ride bareback, the riders have no saddles or **reins**. They have to hold on with their leg muscles.

In bareback riding, the judges watch to make sure the rider's head stays above the horse's shoulders.

7

Around the Arena

The show area is roped off and fenced in. This helps contain the animals and the action. The animals stay in their **chutes** until the contests begin. Then, with the sound of a buzzer or some other signal, the chutes open, and the test of skills begins.

A standard arena is 150 feet by 240 feet (46 m by 73 m). For barrel racing, three barrels are set up. The first two barrels are 60 feet (18 m) from the start and 90 feet (27 m) from each other. The third one is usually 105 feet (32 m) beyond the first two. But in smaller arenas, the lengths can be shorter.

The contestants in barrel races ride around barrels in a path shaped like a cloverleaf.

Big Shows

In the U.S. South, the Houston Livestock Show and Rodeo can bring in as many as 2 million people. In the Northeast, people cheer on bull riders in New York's Madison Square Garden. One of the most popular arenas is the Pit, in Albuquerque, New Mexico. It was named by *Sports Illustrated* as one of the country's top places for sports viewing. The biggest arenas hold the largest crowds. But the majority of rodeos happen in local arenas all around the country, where the fans are much closer to the action.

Each time that a contestant participates in an event, it is called a go-round.

STATE OF RODEO

Before the United States was established, the West was settled by ranchers who moved north from Mexico. Spanish cowboys, called *vaqueros*, used to round up cattle to take to their markets. The U.S. settlers who moved westward followed their traditions.

The word "rodeo" is from the Spanish word *rodear,* which means "to surround."

Working It

From the start, the cowboys would compete to see who was best at their work. The first contests with prizes were held after the Civil War. These events became more popular over time. By the 1980s, more than half of the people in rodeo had never worked on a ranch. Athletes entered the arena from outside the ranching world, and rodeo hit the big time as a sporting event.

New Frontier

Today, rodeo is the official state sport of South Dakota, Texas, and Wyoming. South Dakota has more than 20 major rodeos, and Texas has several big rodeo associations. One of the most famous U.S. rodeos is part of Cheyenne Frontier Days. This Old West celebration happens each July in Cheyenne, Wyoming. The celebration is a blowout of rodeo events, concerts, and carnival rides.

South Dakota

Wyoming

Texas

The country is broken into sections, or circuits, in which rodeo riders compete with one another throughout the year.

11

History and Tradition

The first rodeos featured real cowboys, settling bets about who was the best. By 1900, rodeos were becoming popular with the general public. The early contests were often held along with **Wild West** shows. These shows combined many kinds of acts. There were singers, jugglers, short plays, and people who could perform tricks. They were variety shows with a Wild West theme.

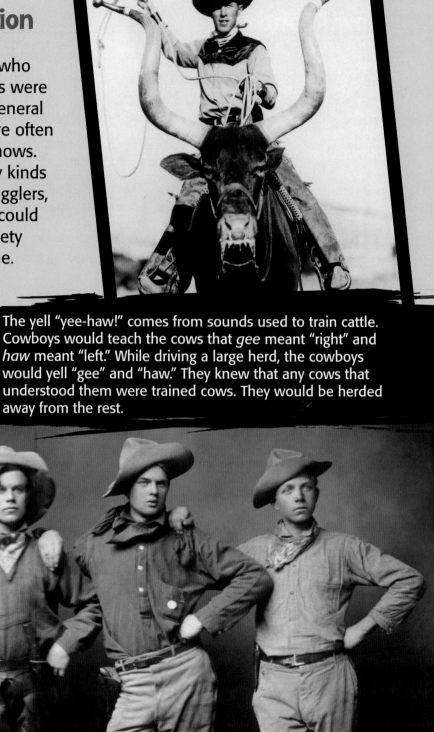

The yell "yee-haw!" comes from sounds used to train cattle. Cowboys would teach the cows that *gee* meant "right" and *haw* meant "left." While driving a large herd, the cowboys would yell "gee" and "haw." They knew that any cows that understood them were trained cows. They would be herded away from the rest.

Trail of Time

1864   The start of rodeo can be traced to this year, when two groups of cowboys met in Deer Trail, Colorado. They wanted to settle a bet on which group was better at roping and riding.

1883   Buffalo Bill's Wild West show formed. Buffalo Bill's real name was William Frederick Cody. He was a Civil War soldier who became an Army scout and then a showman. His show was especially famous.

1897   Cheyenne Frontier Days started in Cheyenne, Wyoming. Today, it is known as the largest outdoor rodeo.

1910   The Pendleton Round-Up began in Pendleton, Oregon.

1929   The first rodeo association formed.

In 1885, Buffalo Bill added Annie Oakley to his show. She led the way for other women in Western sports. By the 1920s, women were common in rodeos in the East. In 1948, the Girl's Rodeo Association formed.

Tough and Rough

At today's rodeos, people see a show that is much like it was a century ago. Rodeo performers show their skills and face down danger. Anyone who looks more closely, however, would see some important differences in safety. Each year, there are one or two deaths at rodeos, and the performers have learned to take steps to protect themselves.

Rodeo is hard on the body, so before training, riders need a full checkup from their doctors.

14

Safe in the Saddle

When rodeo first started, the riders threw themselves into the events. They punished their bodies trying to win. It was a badge of honor to be feeling hurt afterward. But now that rodeo has become more of a sport, there are more safety measures.

The riders wear special vests, which help pad the body, and many bronc and bull riders also wear helmets. They also have mouthpieces to keep from biting their tongues or losing their teeth. Some doctors say that the mouthpieces also cut down the number of **concussions**. They are not sure why this is true, but the gear seems to make the neck and jaw stronger.

Both the riders and the livestock need protection, so the chutes come with safety pads.

GEAR AND STEERS

The equipment used in rodeo includes the saddle, reins, and **riggings**. The gear works best when it is worn in but not worn out. The contestants need to work with various kinds of rope. In rodeo, the quality of rope can make a difference, especially when it comes to bull ropes. The contestants each tend to prefer certain rope handles as well, because the handles have different fits and feels.

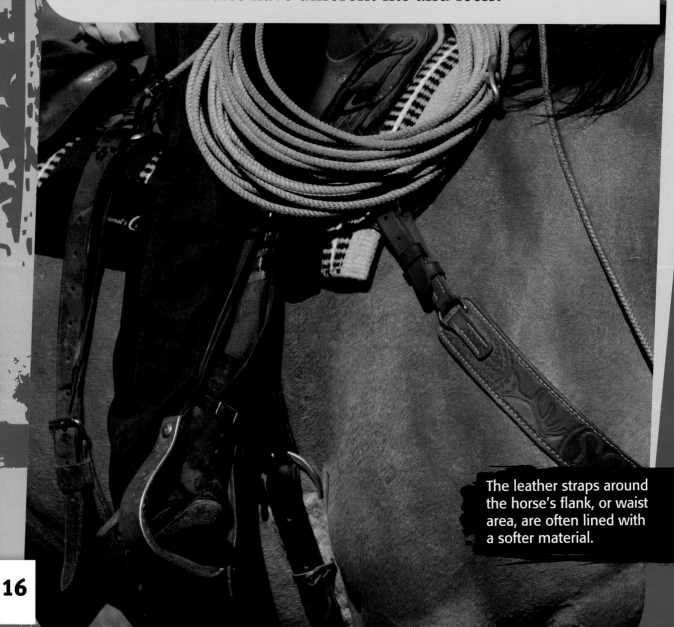

The leather straps around the horse's flank, or waist area, are often lined with a softer material.

Covering the Basics

For roping events, the riders' hands need to be covered with gloves, because the skin on the hand can tear off. Rodeo riders put **rosin** on their gloves to make them work better and help them hold on. The same material is put on the rope where the rope is handled.

TEST IT!

What keeps a **lasso** spinning? Inertia! Try filling a pail halfway with water, and then spin it around to see inertia in action. Inertia is the way a still or moving object resists starting or stopping. An object, such as a spinning pail, will do what it is doing unless something acts on it. The spinning pail will keep moving, and the water will stay in the pail, unless something else forces it to slow down or stop.

Ready to Ride

Ask any cowboy or cowgirl, and he or she will probably say the same thing. The most important thing to wear is a great pair of boots. Cowboy boots have a special shape that makes them good for riding. The toe is narrow, which makes it easier to slip the boot into the **stirrups**. The heel is made to hook on to a stirrup and help the rider stay on as long as possible.

What Do You Think?

Tradition plays a big role in rodeo, and people are proud of the pioneer and Old West qualities of the sport. Think about other sports and their traditions. How are the traditions of rodeo the same or different?

Many riders wear spurs to control the animal's movements. Only dull, spinning spurs are allowed in rodeo. Riders who wear sharp spurs can be fined and thrown out of the competition.

Western Wear

Covering the feet and legs is all part of the cowboy's or cowgirl's winning ways. Chaps are leather leg coverings that go over the rider's jeans. The coverings protect the legs from the rough rides. During a long day of riding, chaps make a difference in comfort.

Cowboy hats have been in use since the mid-1800s.

Hats Off

Cowboy hats have stayed the same because they do the job they were meant to do. The hats are made to keep the sun out of the rider's eyes, and they help keep sweat from the eyes, too. The wide brim and high top also help keep the head cooler on hot days.

Horse Sense

More important than the equipment is the horse that the rider trusts. A good rodeo horse is trained to work with the rider. Even the bucking horses are actually trained to act that way. They are taught to throw riders, using dummy riders made of cloth. Most are trained while young, but older riding horses that are smart are also taught to buck people.

Some horses are better suited to rodeo than others. A rodeo horse must be able to put up with the crowds, the lights, and the noise.

Putting It Together

In some ways, the equipment has improved in rodeo. New materials go into the safety gear, such as the mouthpieces. Today, **electronic eyes** keep track of the riders' starting times, rather than old-fashioned watches. But rodeo's basics remain the same. There is a rider, some gear, and the animals.

A Western saddle has a high front and a high back, with a horn to hold on to. The horse is steered by placing the rein on one side or the other.

TEST IT!

When a horse suddenly stops or changes direction, the rider keeps moving forward. The reason is momentum, or the fact that moving things tend to keep moving even when they are no longer being pushed or pulled. In rodeo and everyday life, an object in motion tends to stay in motion. An object at rest tends to stay at rest.

IN TRAINING

Some cowboys can train for rodeo while on the job, if they work on ranches. They build skills by working day in and out with the animals. But nowadays, rodeo riders more often search for schools that can give them the training they need.

In the Bull Pen

One ranch owner in Washington State allows riders to visit his ranch on Wednesday nights. They test out his bulls, and the animals challenge the riders. Some of the people who line up for this chance at this free training are new to rodeo. Others have been riding in rodeos for a long time and are there for the practice.

To take part in rodeos, even local ones, riders need to buy special insurance, in case they get hurt.

22

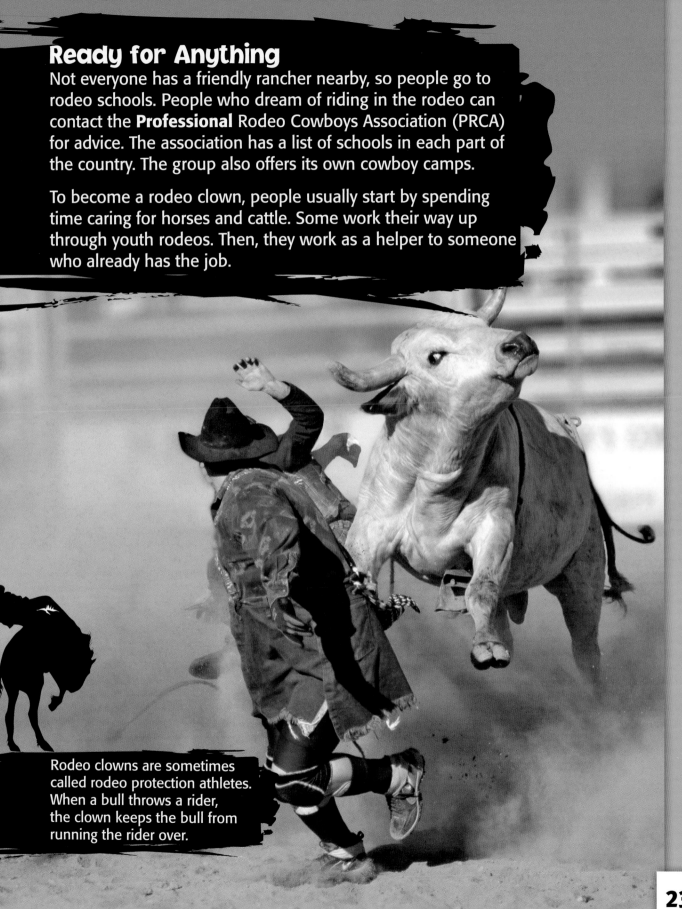

Ready for Anything

Not everyone has a friendly rancher nearby, so people go to rodeo schools. People who dream of riding in the rodeo can contact the **Professional** Rodeo Cowboys Association (PRCA) for advice. The association has a list of schools in each part of the country. The group also offers its own cowboy camps.

To become a rodeo clown, people usually start by spending time caring for horses and cattle. Some work their way up through youth rodeos. Then, they work as a helper to someone who already has the job.

Rodeo clowns are sometimes called rodeo protection athletes. When a bull throws a rider, the clown keeps the bull from running the rider over.

Staying Strong

In olden days, most cowboys would never think to exercise. Just working was enough of a workout. Now, rodeo is like any other sport, and the athletes work to reach the professional level. Many of them train in gyms to stay strong. Even those who are riding for fun exercise their muscles so they can better stay on the horse. As with any other sport, they stay fit by exercising, eating right, and drinking plenty of water.

Aerobic exercise is movement that conditions the heart and lungs. Riders often use aerobic exercise, such as running, to prepare for their performances.

Traditional Training

Training in a gym will take a would-be rodeo rider only so far, however. The hardworking riders also train with traditional methods. One of the tools of training is an exercise machine called a bucking barrel. Basically, it is a barrel that hangs between posts on springs. By climbing aboard, the rider can get used to staying in balance. But nothing replaces practice on the real thing.

Being strong in both the upper and lower body lowers the risk of injury.

TEST IT!

One of the laws of motion says that for every action there is an equal and opposite reaction. In other words, all forces come in pairs. For example, when a cowboy jumps on a bucking barrel, it springs down and then it springs up. To think about action-reaction pairs, flip through this book. Look at all the times that something is about to happen in the pictures. Think through to what is going to happen next.

SHOWTIME!

The excitement kicks off with the grand entry, when the riders enter the arena carrying flags and banners. The American flag is raised, and the crowd sings "The Star-Spangled Banner." Then, it is time for the events. Who will win? Who will fall?

Buzz of Excitement

The lineup of events changes from one rodeo to another. In a high school rodeo, the riders might compete in a pole bending competition. When the buzzer goes off, it is like a shock of excitement. A horse and rider pass through a line of poles and then turn back and weave back and forth through them.

Pole racing features six poles in a straight line. They are 21 feet apart.

Crowd Pleasers

The main event at professional rodeos is bull riding, in which the rider mounts a bull instead of a horse. It is a lot like watching bareback riding on horses, but way more dangerous. The bulls have been trained to fight the riders, and the animals are enormous.

Each event brings its own excitement. There is usually a break in the middle with entertainment, such as a singer, a band, or a clown act. Many of the clowns have other jobs, such as being there to help if a rider falls. At a rodeo, sports, entertainment, and tradition come together as they do nowhere else.

Some of the large associations in rodeo are dedicated only to bull riding.

Buckle Up

At youth rodeos, the riders can win **trophies**, medals, and ribbons. Everyone can go home with a pin for participation. But the big prize at most rodeos is something that is special to this sport—the trophy buckle.

Belt buckles are made in honor of many rodeos, as a way for people to remember the day. But the trophy buckle is a special prize made of silver, gold, or other valued materials. The most prized belt buckle in rodeo is for All-Around Cowboy, given by the PRCA.

Everyday belt buckles often show something about family history, such as the name of a family ranch. Trophy buckles are signs of accomplishment.

Time and Points

Rodeos have both timed events and rough stock events. The timed events, such as pole bending, are run like a race with the clock. But in rough stock, the number of points decides who wins. Points are given to both the animal and the rider, and the animal's points are added to those of the rider. This is a way to count for the fact that the animals put up more of a fight sometimes. The tougher the animal, the more points it gets.

The rough stock events are the most dangerous. They include bronc and bull riding.

TEST IT!

In rough stock, you add the points for the animal and rider together to get the rider's final points. In which case below is the outcome better for the rider?

1. A bull gets a score of 30, and a rider gets a score of 22.

2. A bull gets a score of 41, and a rider gets a score of 11.

Answer: Even though the first rider got twice as many points as the second, the outcome is the same. Both riders ended up with a score of 52.

Make the Association

The most well-known association for rodeo is the PRCA. But in areas where there are plenty of ranches, there are rodeo groups at the local and state levels. Some of these associations are organized by ages. For example, there are rodeos for children, high school students, college students, and senior citizens.

Many rodeos also have prizes besides buckles and other trophies. At a high school contest, the top prize may be a new saddle. At rodeos for adults, people may ride to win a new truck or money.

All Together
The associations represent the riders. They also help the people who train the animals, judge the events, and work at the shows and behind the scenes. There is also a group called the Women's Professional Rodeo Association. Women have been participating since the early 1900s, especially in trick riding.

Trick riding involves the stunts that are done for show. The trick riders no longer compete for rodeo prizes. The tricks became far too dangerous to continue as sports competition.

ALL-AROUND STARS

The National Finals Rodeo is held each December to crown the best athletes and performers. It is the final event of the season for the PRCA. This famous rodeo has been held in Las Vegas at the University of Nevada. It is like the Super Bowl of rodeo.

Best of the Rest

The top riders of the season are invited to compete for the world titles. They battle each other in the main events. The top finishers share millions of dollars in winnings, and one of the winners is named the All-Around Cowboy.

Follow the Money

The PRCA has the most prize money of any rodeo group. But rodeos of all sizes offer prize money. Most towns have an association of its businesses. These groups often put up the prize money for the local events.

Some prize money comes from the entry fees paid by the people who compete. But most of it comes from businesses and other leaders. Rodeo is an exciting event that brings people in the community together. It also attracts visitors, so it is natural for businesspeople to want to see their rodeo be a success.

The National Cowgirl Museum and Hall of Fame, in Fort Worth, Texas, is dedicated to "women who shaped the West," including rodeo riders.

Stars Shine

Each generation has its own rodeo stars. In the 1930s, one such star was Hoot Gibson, who not only won championships but became a movie star. Today, a popular star is Trevor Brazile, who was named All-Around Cowboy many times in a row. It is not only the riders who are famous. In 2002 and 2003, a bull from North Dakota was named the Best Bucking Bull in the rodeo tour. His name was Little Yellow Jacket, and he had some big fans. People were excited to see him.

The horses are stars in their own right. Videos of the horses get shown online the way that parents show off pictures of their babies.

Star Projects

Rodeo is exciting, and that energy is often used to bring attention to charities. For example, the Houston Livestock Show and Rodeo gives **scholarships** to students. Some rodeos benefit groups such as the Future Farmers of America or people who served in the military. The money raised feeds the hungry or sends kids to camps. Many rodeos raise money for causes such as the American Cancer Society, the American Heart Association, and animal rescue groups. In this way, the winning riders bring in a win for others as well.

Some rodeos raise money to research livestock. The researchers look for new medicines and other improvements for the animals.

Animal Spirits

Rodeos raise people's spirits while raising money for special causes, but some people think that rodeos should not be allowed to operate. Some animal rights groups say that the cows, bulls, and horses should not be used for entertainment.

Rodeo athletes risk being hurt, and the animals bear some risk as well. Some people think rodeos should be shut down for this reason. Others point to the fact that rodeo animals live longer and have better medical care than livestock. Where do you stand on this issue? Can you think of pros and cons to add to this list?

Pros
Animals in rodeos are cared for and well fed. If they lived in nature, they would be more likely to get hurt.

Rodeos bring people close to livestock. The events teach people about the beauty and power of the animals.

Cons
Animals are raised to work in rodeos, so they do not have a chance to be in the wild, which might make them happier.

The performers are fined for hurting animals, but no one keeps track of all the animals that are hurt.

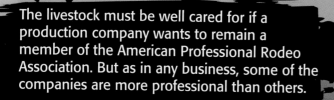

The livestock must be well cared for if a production company wants to remain a member of the American Professional Rodeo Association. But as in any business, some of the companies are more professional than others.

In response to the animal rights groups, rodeo leaders have taken extra steps to protect the livestock. Some kinds of equipment have been forbidden, such as straps that hurt the animals. Do you think this is enough?

37

TEAM SPORT

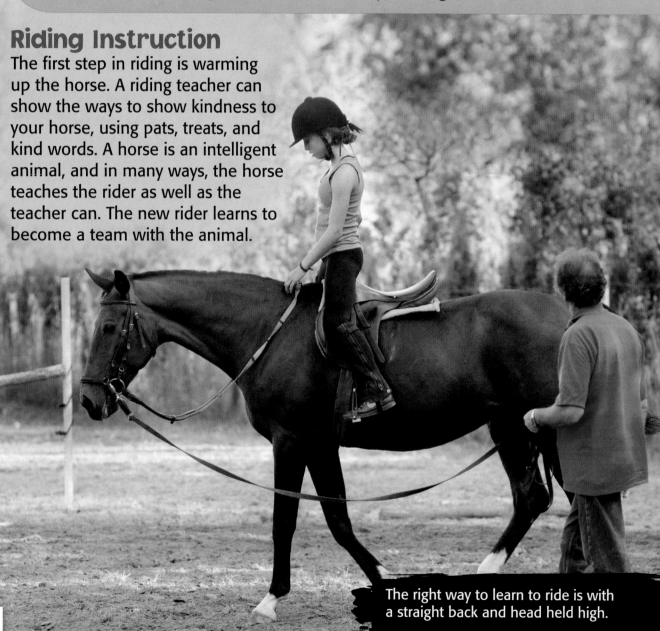

Can you see yourself on a horse, riding in an arena and chasing down a steer? Would-be rodeo stars first have to learn to ride a horse. It all starts by learning to build trust between a rider and a horse. Many times, the people who teach riding will encourage new riders to try riding without a saddle.

Riding Instruction

The first step in riding is warming up the horse. A riding teacher can show the ways to show kindness to your horse, using pats, treats, and kind words. A horse is an intelligent animal, and in many ways, the horse teaches the rider as well as the teacher can. The new rider learns to become a team with the animal.

The right way to learn to ride is with a straight back and head held high.

Mount the Effort

Using treats, you make sure the horse can open his or her mouth to accept the bridle. This is the headgear used to control the horse. The teacher shows you how to saddle up and how to get on and off the back of the animal. This is called mounting and dismounting. You go through paces with the animal, learning to go and stop faster with each practice.

A rider learns to exercise the horse's head, neck, and legs. This helps the horse stay healthy and helps the rider win its trust.

Taking the Reins

Buying a horse is a huge cost, and so is buying or renting space to keep it. Owning a horse is too expensive for most people. But you do not need to own one to learn to ride. You can start by taking lessons at parks and at schools. Later, you can try renting a horse and equipment. If you enjoy riding, you can also think about getting into **dressage**. That is another way to compete as a rider, which is less dangerous than rodeo.

Riders wear helmets for advanced horseback riding for the same reasons that people wear helmets while riding on bikes and motorcycles.

Learning the Ropes

To ride in the rodeo, you need to be able to handle a horse. You also need to know your way around other livestock, so look for ways to work with animals. Find jobs and classes on ranches and farms, so you can learn how the animals act and think.

To learn roping, riders first try roping dummies and other objects. In time, they try roping from a moving horse. When you are ready, you can contact the PRCA to find the nearest rodeo teachers.

You can see where your interest takes you.

TALKING LIKE A RODEO RIDER

Rodeo has its own special language to describe the acts and the animals. Some of the words used in rodeo sound just like their meaning. The word "dink" means "a small animal." An "arm jerker" is a horse or bull that is very powerful. "Breaking the barrier" is what happens when an animal breaks through the starting rope before it has opened.

On Their Terms

Many of the sayings are colorful. For example, no one wants to be "freight trained." That means getting run over by a bull that is running as fast as possible. *Chasing the cans* is another name for barrel racing. Many rodeo terms are easy enough to understand when you hear them in use. But others are harder to guess. For example, a *hooey* is the name of a knot used to tie an animal's feet.

Words in Context

Can you guess the meaning of these rodeo words and phrases?

1. They called her *High Roller*, and that horse really lives up to her name.

    high roller: an animal that leaps high when bucking

2. That bull threw him *out the backdoor*.

    out the backdoor: from the back of the animal

3. When he was riding in the third event, you could *see daylight*.

    see daylight: when a rider flies so far from the horse that people see light between the rider and the animal

LEGENDS OF RODEO

The legends of rodeo are men and women whose skills and daring won attention and awards. Some are pioneers of the sport, and others are record breakers. In many cases, they have used their stardom to help others.

Five Famous Rodeo Riders

In 1905, **Lucille Mulhall** performed in a rodeo at Madison Square Garden at age 10. She is often called "America's First Cowgirl."

Florence Hughes Randolph won the Metro Goldwyn Mayer Trophy in 1927. It was given to the top female in rodeo at the Madison Square Garden World Series Rodeo. Randolph was famous for being able to do a backward somersault from one horse to another.

Ty Murray was named to the Rodeo Hall of Fame in 2000. He was the PRCA World Champion nine times and the All-Around Cowboy seven times.

Denny Flynn was inducted into the Professional Bull Riders Ring of Honor in 2002, and in 2010 he entered the ProRodeo Hall of Fame for Lifetime Achievement.

Flint Rasmussen won the PRCA Clown of the Year award eight years in a row.

Behind the Legends

Several states and various groups have a hall of fame for rodeo legends. In Colorado Springs, Colorado, the ProRodeo Hall of Fame has honored more than 200 people, and more than 25 animals, since opening in 1979. Winners are chosen in one of several categories. Here are some examples.

category	year	person or animal
contestant	1979	**Warren G. "Freckles" Brown**, a bull rider and World War II hero
stock contractor	1979	**Gene Autry**, an actor in movie Westerns, who raised rodeo animals in Colorado after leaving Hollywood
livestock	1979	**Bullet**, a horse who carried his owners to five world titles

Looking for More

Would you like to win a buckle in rodeo history? You can use your library, and the Internet, to research people and animals who made a name for themselves in rodeo. Find out where they lived. Learn what records they hold. A selection of names follows. But you can also research other legends.

name	short description
Annie Oakley	famous female performer in Buffalo Bill's Wild West and Congress of Rough Riders of the World
Fannie Sperry Steele	first woman named to the Rodeo Hall of Fame
Baby Doll	a horse that was one of the first named to the Rodeo Hall of Fame
Robert and Billy Etbauer	brothers who were honored together by the Rodeo Hall of Fame after retiring from the sport
Bill Pickett	pioneer of the rodeo steer wrestling event who had to work against racial prejudice as a black rodeo star

Glossary

broncing: bucking; trying to throw the rider

chutes: tubes or channels

concussions: injuries to the brain from a blow or fall

dressage: a show of animal training in which a horse makes exact movements in response to a rider's hidden commands

electronic eyes: devices used to measure light and to use those measurements to keep time or record images

lasso: long rope with a running knot or noose on one end, used for catching livestock

livestock: farm animals, including cattle

professional: in sports, having to do with athletes who are paid or sponsored

reins: straps at either end of the bridle, which fits around the animal's head

riggings: equipment used to control, operate, and guide a horse

rosin: material taken from the stumps or sap of pine trees

saddle bronc: event in which a horse tries to throw a rider from the saddle

scholarships: awards given to students to further their education

steer: male ox or related animal

stirrups: loops or rings on either side of a saddle which support the foot

trophies: things gained in victory, such as fancy objects

Wild West: western United States during the period of time when it was being settled and law had not yet been established

For More Information

Books

Branzei, Sylvia. *Rebel in a Dress: Cowgirls.* Philadelphia, PA: Running Press Kids, 2011.

Broyles, Matthew. *Pole Bending.* New York, NY: Rosen Central, 2006.

Kubke, Jane. *Bull Riding.* New York, NY: Rosen Central, 2006.

Kupperberg, Paul. *Rodeo Clowns.* New York, NY: Rosen Central, 2006.

Websites

The Library of Congress
www.loc.gov/index.html
The Library of Congress, known as "America's Memory," has a collection of photos, songs, and much more that illustrate rodeo's role in American history. Enter "rodeo" in the search box.

National Cowboy & Western Heritage Museum
www.nationalcowboymuseum.org/
The National Cowboy & Western Heritage Museum features the Diamond Ranch, an online exhibit with information for students, including cowboy songs and games.

Professional Rodeo Cowboys Association
www.prorodeo.com/
The Professional Rodeo Cowboys Association offers rodeo news, the standings, and highlights of events.

Index